LOVING GOD THROUGH THE DARKNESS

Selected Writings of
JOHN OF THE CROSS

Upper Room Spiritual Classics® — Series 3

Selected, edited, and introduced by
Keith Beasley-Topliffe

UPPER
ROOM BOOKS™
NASHVILLE

Loving God through the Darkness:
Selected Writings of John of the Cross

The Upper Room® Website: http://www.upperroom.org

UPPER ROOM,® UPPER ROOM BOOKS™ and design logos are trademarks owned by the Upper Room,® Nashville, Tennessee. All rights reserved.

Scripture quotations are from the New Revised Standard Version of the Bible Copyright © 1989 by the Division of Christian Education of the National Council of Churches of Christ in the USA. Used by permission. All rights reserved.

Excerpts from *The Collected Works of St. John of the Cross* translated by Kieran Kavanaugh and Otilio Rodriquez 1979, 1991, by Washington Province of Discalced Carmelites. ICS Publications, 2131 Lincoln Road, N.E., Washington, D.C. 20002, U.S.A.

Cover design: Gore Studio, Inc.
Interior design and layout: Nancy J. Cole

First printing: 2000

Library of Congress Cataloging-in-Publication Data

John of the Cross, Saint, 1542–1591.
  [Selections. English. 2000]
  Loving God through the darkness : selected writings of John of the Cross / selected, edited, and introduced by Keith Beasley-Topliffe.
      p. cm. — (Upper Room spiritual classics. Series 3)
  ISBN 0-8358-0904-8
  1. Spiritual life—Catholic Church. I. Beasley-Topliffe, Keith.
II. Title. III. Series.
BX2179.J63213 2000   99-37741
248.2'2—dc21   CIP

Printed in the United States of America

TABLE OF CONTENTS

INTRODUCTION

When we are beginning to grow as Christians, our love of God is inevitably mixed up with other loves. We love other people, our country, our possessions. We love the blessings God gives us, even the good feelings we get from prayer.

If we are to continue to grow, we must become detached from these loves so that we can move toward loving God alone. John of the Cross, a Carmelite monk who lived in Spain during the sixteenth century, described this process of detachment as a dark night of the soul. This night has both active and passive aspects: things we do to lay aside attachments and things God does in our souls to wean us from them. He uses biblical stories and vivid metaphors to explain both the process and the need for it, offering guidance for beginners and those far along the spiritual path.

JOHN'S WORLD

Spain in the sixteenth century was a nation in turmoil. Granada, the last Moorish stronghold, fell in 1492. A land where Jew, Christian, and Muslim once lived together fairly peacefully became exclusively Christian. Jews and Muslims had to leave or convert. Thirteen years earlier, the Spanish Inquisition had been formed, in part, to test the sincerity of such forced conversions and weed out all whose faith did not conform to official Roman Catholic teachings.

After the beginnings of the Protestant Reformation in 1517, the Inquisition also examined any who insisted on the primacy of grace or the priesthood of all believers. On the other hand, the Spanish king was interested in church reform, particularly reform movements in monastic orders. Innovative spiritual leaders could find themselves in the midst of the ongoing power struggle between church and crown.

The Carmelite Order to which John belonged began with a group of pilgrims who founded a community on Mount Carmel in the Holy Land near the beginning of the thirteenth century. When Muslim victories forced them to leave, they brought their way of life back to Western Europe. They were granted recognition in 1247 as an order dedicated to prayer and teaching. A few years later, the Order of Carmelite Sisters began. Both orders spread through France, Spain, Italy, and England. In 1562, Teresa of Avila, a Carmelite nun, began a reform movement, establishing new Carmelite convents with a stricter observance of the order's rule and a greater emphasis on prayer. Because one aspect of their stricter rule was wearing sandals rather than shoes, they were called "discalced," or shoeless. Six years later Teresa was ready to extend the reform to the men. John was one of the three monks in the first monastery established.

John was highly educated and his writings reflect his learning. Of particular importance for his descriptions of the spiritual life is the understanding of the mind, described in terms of faculties. According to John, the mind has three primary (or higher) faculties: the will, the intellect, and the memory, all operating more or less independently. Together these form the human spirit. So John can talk of the will being united to God while the intellect is distracted by many thoughts. When the memory and the intellect are quieted and brought back into alignment with the will, this is "recollection." These primary faculties were supported by the five exterior senses as well as three interior ones. *Phantasy* forms internal images based on external or supernatural sensory impressions. *Sense memory* stores such impressions and images. *Imagination* uses these images to form new images for things not directly experienced. Learning to ignore the constant clamor of all these senses is another, more basic sort of recollection. John's distinction between the purification of the senses and the purification of the spirit is based on this understanding.

JOHN'S LIFE

John was born as Juan de Yepes in 1542 in Fontiveros, Castile. He was the third son of Gonzalo de Yepes and Catalina Alvarez. Gonzalo had been disinherited by his wealthy silk merchant father for marrying beneath his station. When he died, two years after John's birth, Catalina's trade as a weaver kept the family alive, even if in grave poverty. The middle brother, Luis, died when John was five, and John remained small (an inch less than five feet tall and thin) for his whole life.

When the family moved to Medina del Campo, John was able to study at a local school for orphans. After showing little promise in other trades, John began to help out in a hospital. The administrator recognized his intelligence and caring and arranged for him to study further with the Jesuits while continuing to assist at the hospital. When he was twenty-one (1563, the year after the beginning of Teresa's reform), John became a novice in the Carmelite Order, taking the name John of Saint Matthias. Following his final vows, he was sent to the University of Salamanca for four years. In 1567 he was ordained and returned to Medina to celebrate his first Mass. Teresa was in town, establishing her second Medina convent. When they met, John decided to join her reform. John was twenty-five years old, Teresa fifty-two. After completing his education, he went to Valladolid for several months to learn from Teresa.

On November 28, 1568, John and two others started the first friars' house of the reform. John was subprior and novice master and took the new name John of the Cross. Over the next few years he worked to establish the reform. In 1572, Teresa was recalled to her home convent in Avila to be prioress. She asked John to be vicar and confessor for the convent as well as her own spiritual director.

In 1575, the General Chapter of the Carmelite Order, meeting in Italy and without benefit of leaders from Spain, demanded an end to the reform and the return of all discalced Carmelites into the regular Carmelite houses. With the Spanish king Philip II supporting the reform, John continued at Avila, ignoring the demand. On December 2, 1577, though, he was abducted and taken to the Carmelite monastery in Toledo where he was confined in a six-by-ten-foot room for about nine months. He spent his time in prayer and in composing poetry about the love between the soul and God. Eventually a new jailer allowed him pen and ink to write down the poems. In August 1578, he decided to escape. John loosened the screws of the lock until one night he was able to break the door open, run down the hall to a window, and escape by means of a rope made from torn mattress covers. Friends got him to safety in Andalusia (southern Spain), where the Carmelite leadership was more sympathetic to the reform. John became vicar of a discalced monastery, El Calvario in Sierra del Segura. There he continued to offer spiritual direction to people from all walks of life and to write poetry (including the poem "One Dark Night"). He also planned and started a discalced college in Baeza where he served as rector from 1579 to 1582. During that time Teresa's reform was officially confirmed by the pope, and the discalced were free to establish new houses for men and women.

In 1582 (a few months before Teresa's death) John became prior of Los Martires in Granada. There he designed the monastery gardens and an aqueduct for the monastery. Over the course of the next six years he wrote four books on the spiritual life as prolonged commentaries on his poems. Two were on "One Dark Night" and the others were on "The Spiritual Canticle" and "The Living Flame of Love." In 1585 he became vicar provincial for Andalusia and spent much of his time overseeing new foundations.

In 1588, John became prior in Segovia. Three years later, after a disagreement over the governing of the order, John was removed from all offices. He offered to go to Mexico, but first went to La Penuela in the mountains of Andalusia. After a couple of months, he became ill. In September 1591, John went to the discalced house in Ubeda for medical care. He died there on December 14, just after the stroke of midnight. He was canonized in 1726. Two hundred years later Pope Pius XI declared him a Doctor of the Church.

FURTHER READING

The Collected Works of Saint John of the Cross, translated by Kieran Kavanaugh and Otilio Rodriguez (rev. ed. ICS Publications, 1991), is the best modern translation and the basis for these selections. More extensive selections from this translation are available in the Paulist Press volume on John of the Cross. Some of the main works are also available as separate paperbacks from Image Books in an older translation by E. Allison Peers.

The best short biography and introduction to John is the introduction to the Kavanaugh and Rodriguez translation. Two books by Susan Muto offer excellent commentary to help modern readers understand John's teaching: *John of the Cross for Today: The Ascent* and *John of the Cross for Today: The Dark Night*, both from Ave Maria Press.

The works of Teresa of Avila (also translated by Kavanaugh and Rodriguez and available from ICS Publications) are the ideal complement to reading John of the Cross. Other important influences on John include Bernard of Clairvaux, Thomas Aquinas, and Francisco de Osuna.

NOTE ON THE TEXT

These selections are taken from the Kavanaugh and Rodriguez translations of *The Ascent of Mount Carmel* and *The Dark Night of the Soul*. They have been edited primarily for length. Scripture quotations have been conformed to the New Revised Standard Version where possible.

ONE DARK NIGHT

John wrote this poem shortly after his escape from imprisonment in 1578. His two treatises on the dark night of the soul begin as commentaries on the poem, although John never gets beyond the third stanza. Note that the Spanish words translated "Lover" and "Beloved" are the masculine and feminine forms of the same adjective and do not imply the active and passive connotations of the English words.

Songs of the soul that rejoices in having reached the high state of perfection, which is union with God, by the path of spiritual negation.

> One dark night,
> fired with love's urgent longings
> —ah, the sheer grace!—
> I went out unseen,
> my house being now all stilled.
>
> In darkness and secure,
> by the secret ladder, disguised,
> —ah, the sheer grace!—
> in darkness and concealment,
> my house being now all stilled.
>
> On that glad night,
> in secret, for no one saw me,
> nor did I look at anything,
> with no other light or guide
> than the one that burned in my heart.

This guided me
more surely than the light of noon
to where he was awaiting me
—him I knew so well—
there in a place where no one appeared.

O guiding night!
O night more lovely than the dawn!
O night that has united
the Lover with his Beloved,
transforming the Beloved in her Lover.

Upon my flowering breast
which I kept wholly for him alone,
there he lay sleeping,
and I caressing him
there in a breeze from the fanning cedars.

When the breeze blew from the turret,
as I parted his hair,
it wounded my neck
with its gentle hand,
suspending all my senses.

I abandoned and forgot myself,
laying my face on my Beloved;
all things ceased; I went out from myself,
leaving my cares
forgotten among the lilies.

JOHN'S PURPOSE IN WRITING

From *The Ascent of Mount Carmel*, Prologue,
Sections 3–8

---

*About 1579, John created a sketch of "The Mount of
Perfection" that showed the "negative path" of self-denial he
taught. The Ascent of Mount Carmel, written a year or so
later, begins as a commentary on both the sketch and the
poem "The Dark Night." In this introductory passage, John
explains the need for understanding the dark night of the
soul, especially on the part of spiritual directors.*

I am not undertaking this arduous task because of
any particular confidence in my own abilities. Rather,
I am confident that the Lord will help me explain this
matter because it is extremely necessary to so many
souls. Even though these souls have begun to walk
along the road of virtue, and our Lord desires to place
them in the dark night that they may move on to the
divine union, they do not advance. The reason for this
may be that sometimes they do not want to enter the
dark night or allow themselves to be placed in it, or
that sometimes they misunderstand themselves and
are without suitable and alert directors who will show
them the way to the summit. God gives many souls
the talent and grace for advancing, and should they
desire to make the effort they would arrive at this
high state. And so it is sad to see them continue in

their lowly method of communion with God because they do not want or know how to advance, or because they receive no direction on breaking away from the methods of beginners. Even if our Lord finally comes to their aid to the extent of making them advance without these helps, they reach the summit much later, expend more effort, and gain less merit, because they do not willingly adapt themselves to God's work of placing them on the pure and reliable road leading to union. Although God does lead them—since he can do so without their cooperation—they do not accept his guidance. In resisting God who is conducting them, they make little progress and fail in merit because they do not apply their wills; as a result they must endure greater suffering. Some souls, instead of abandoning themselves to God and cooperating with him, hamper him by their indiscreet activity or their resistance. They resemble children who kick and cry and struggle to walk by themselves when their mothers want to carry them; in walking by themselves they make no headway, or if they do, it is at a child's pace.

With God's help, then, we will propose doctrine and counsel for beginners and proficients that they may understand or at least know how to practice abandonment to God's guidance when he wants them to advance.

It will happen to individuals that while they are being conducted by God along a sublime path of dark contemplation and aridity, in which they feel lost and filled with darknesses, trials, conflicts, and temptations, they will meet someone who, in the style of Job's comforters, will proclaim that all of this is due to melancholia, depression, or temperament, or to some hidden wickedness, and that as a result God has forsaken them. Therefore the usual verdict is that these individuals must have lived an evil life since such trials afflict them.

Other directors will tell them that they are falling back since they find no satisfaction or consolation as they previously did in the things of God. Such talk only doubles the trial of a poor soul. It will happen that the soul's greatest suffering will be caused by the knowledge of its own miseries. That it is full of evil and sin is as clear as day to it, and even clearer, for, as we shall say further on, God is the author of this enlightenment in the night of contemplation. And when this soul finds someone who agrees with what it feels (that these trials are all its own fault), its suffering and distress grow without bounds. And this suffering usually becomes worse than death.

With divine help we will discuss all this: how individuals should behave; what method the confessor should use in dealing with them; signs to recognize this purification of the soul that we call the dark night; whether it is the purification of the senses or of the spirit; and how we can discern whether this affliction is caused by melancholia or some other deficiency of sense or spirit.

Some souls or their confessors may think that God is leading them along this road of the dark night of spiritual purgation, but perhaps this will not be so.

What they suffer will be due to one of these deficiencies. Likewise, many individuals think they are not praying when, indeed, their prayer is deep. Others place high value on their prayer while it amounts to little more than nothing.

Some people—and it is sad to see them—work and tire themselves greatly, and yet go backward; they look for progress in what brings no progress but instead hinders them. Others, in peace and tranquillity, continue to advance well. Some others let themselves be encumbered by the very consolations and favors God bestows on them for the sake of their advancing, and they advance not at all.

We will also discuss many other experiences of those who walk along this road: joys, afflictions, hopes, and sorrows—some of these originating from the spirit of perfection, others from the spirit of imperfection. Our goal will be to explain, with God's help, all these points so that those who read this book will in some way discover the road they are walking along, and the one they ought to follow if they want to reach the summit of this mount.

Readers should not be surprised if this doctrine on the dark night—through which a soul advances toward God—appears somewhat obscure. This, I believe, will be the case as they begin to read, but as they read on they will understand it better since the latter parts will explain the former. Then, if they read this work a second time, the matter will seem clearer and the doctrine sounder.

# LIGHT AND DARK

In this selection, John explains the importance of stripping away all worldly attachments.

The necessity to pass through this dark night (the mortification of the appetites and denial of pleasure in all things) to attain divine union with God arises from the fact that all of a person's attachments to creatures are pure darkness in God's sight. Clothed in these affections, people are incapable of the enlightenment and dominating fullness of God's pure and simple light.

The reason, as we learn in philosophy, is that two contraries cannot coexist in the same subject. Darkness, which is an attachment to creatures, and light, which is God, are contraries and bear no likeness toward each other, as Saint Paul teaches in his letter to the Corinthians, "What fellowship is there between light and darkness?" Consequently, the light of divine union cannot be established in the soul until these affections are eradicated.

For a better proof of this, it ought to be kept in mind that an attachment to a creature makes a person equal to that creature; the stronger the attachment, the closer is the likeness to the creature and the greater the equality, for love effects a likeness between the lover and the beloved. Anyone who loves a creature, then, is as low as that creature and in some way even lower because love not only equates but even subjects the lover to the loved creature.

All creatures of heaven and earth are nothing when compared to God, as Jeremiah points out: "I looked on the earth, and lo, it was waste and void; and to the heavens, and they had no light." By saying that he saw an empty earth, he meant that all its creatures were nothing and that the earth too was nothing. In stating that he looked up to the heavens and beheld no light, he meant that all the heavenly luminaries were pure darkness in comparison to God. All creatures considered in this way are nothing, and a person's attachments to them are less than nothing since these attachments are an impediment to and deprive the soul of transformation in God—just as darkness is nothing and less than nothing since it is a privation of light. In no way, then, is such a person capable of union with the infinite being of God. There is no likeness between what is not and what is. To be particular, here are some examples.

All the beauty of creatures compared to the infinite beauty of God is the height of ugliness. As Solomon says in Proverbs: "Charm is deceitful, and beauty is vain." So a person attached to the beauty of any creature is extremely ugly in God's sight. A soul so unsightly is incapable of transformation into the beauty that is God.

All the grace and elegance of creatures compared to God's grace is utter coarseness and crudity.

That is why a person captivated by this grace and elegance of creatures becomes highly coarse and crude in God's sight. Someone like this is incapable of the infinite grace and beauty of God.

Compared to the infinite goodness of God, all the goodness of the creatures of the world can be called wickedness. Nothing is good but God alone. Those who set their hearts on the good things of the world become extremely wicked in the sight of God. Since wickedness does not comprehend goodness, such persons will be incapable of union with God, who is supreme goodness.

All the world's wisdom compared to the wisdom of God is pure and utter ignorance, as Saint Paul writes to the Corinthians: "God's foolishness is wiser than human wisdom." Those, therefore, who value their knowledge and ability as a means of reaching union with the wisdom of God are highly ignorant in God's sight and will be left behind, far away from this wisdom. Ignorance does not grasp what wisdom is. In God's sight those who think they have some wisdom are very ignorant. The Apostle says of them in writing to the Romans: "Claiming to be wise, they became fools."

Only those who set aside their own knowledge and walk in God's service like unlearned children receive wisdom from God. This is the wisdom about which Saint Paul taught the Corinthians: "If you think that you are wise in this age, you should become fools so that you may become wise." Accordingly, to reach union with the wisdom of God, a person must advance by unknowing rather than by knowing.

All the delights and satisfactions of the will in the things of the world compared to all the delight that is God are intense suffering, torment, and bitterness. Those who link their hearts to these delights, then, deserve in God's eyes intense suffering, torment, and bitterness. They will not be capable of attaining the delights of the embrace of union with God, since they merit suffering and bitterness.

All the wealth and glory of creation compared to the wealth that is God is utter poverty and misery in the Lord's sight. The person who loves and possesses these things is completely poor and miserable before God and will be unable to attain the richness and glory of transformation in God.

Divine Wisdom, with pity for these souls that become ugly, abject, miserable, and poor because of their love for worldly things, which in their opinion are rich and beautiful, exclaims in Proverbs: "To you, O people, I call, and my cry is to all that live. O simple ones, learn prudence; acquire intelligence, you who lack it. Hear, for I will speak noble things . . . Riches and honor are with me, enduring wealth and prosperity. My fruit is better than gold, even fine gold, and my yield than choice silver. I walk in the way of righteousness, along the paths of justice, endowing with wealth those who love me, and filling their treasuries."

Divine Wisdom speaks, here, to all those who are attached to the things of the world. She tells them that she is dealing with great things, not small things, as they are. The riches and glory they love are with her and in her, not where they think. Lofty riches and justice are present in her. Although in their opinion the things of this world are riches, she tells them to bear in mind that her riches are more precious, that the fruit found in them will be better than gold and precious stones, and that what she begets in souls has greater value than cherished silver, which signifies every kind of affection possible in this life.

# dETACHMENT

From *The Ascent of Mount Carmel*, Book 1, Chapter 5,
Sections 3–8

*In this passage, John uses several biblical examples as alle-
gories of the spiritual need for detachment before we can be
open to receive God's blessings.*

We have a figure of this in Exodus where we read that
God did not give the children of Israel the heavenly
manna until they exhausted the flour brought from
Egypt. The meaning here is that first a total renuncia-
tion is needed, for this bread of angels is disagreeable
to the palate of anyone who wants to taste human
food. Persons feeding on other strange tastes not only
become incapable of the divine Spirit, but even greatly
anger the divine Majesty because in their aspirations
for spiritual food they are not satisfied with God alone,
but mix with these aspirations a desire and affection
for other things. This is likewise apparent in the same
book of sacred Scripture where it states that the
people, discontented with that simple food, requested
and craved meat, and seriously angered our Lord
because of their desire to commingle a food so base
and coarse with one so high and simple that, even
though simple, contained the savor and substance of
all foods. Consequently, while morsels of manna were
yet in their mouths, the wrath of God descended on

them, as David also says, spouting fire from heaven and reducing thousands of them to ashes. For God thought it shameful for them to crave other food while he was giving them heavenly food.

Oh, if spiritual persons knew how much spiritual good and abundance they lose by not attempting to raise their appetites above childish things, and if they knew to what extent, by not desiring the taste of these trifles, they would discover in this simple spiritual food the savor of all things! The Israelites did not perceive the taste of every other food that was contained in the manna, because their appetite was not centered on this manna alone. They were unsuccessful in deriving from the manna all the taste and strength they were looking for, not because the manna didn't have these but because of their craving for other foods. Similarly, those who love something together with God undoubtedly make little of God, for they weigh in the balance with God an object far distant from God, as we have said.

This was also indicated when God ordered Moses to climb to the top of the mountain. He did this that Moses might be able to speak to him. He commanded Moses not only to ascend alone and leave the children of Israel below, but to rule against even the pasturing of beasts on the mountainside. The meaning is that those who ascend this mount of perfection to converse with God must not only renounce all things by leaving them at the bottom, but also restrict their appetites (the beasts) from pasturing on the mountainside, on things that are not purely God. For in God, or in the state of perfection, all appetites cease.

We also have a striking figure of this in Genesis. When the patriarch Jacob desired to ascend Mount Bethel to build an altar to offer sacrifice to God, he first ordered his people to do three things: destroy all strange gods; purify themselves; and change their garments.

Those desiring to climb to the summit of the mount in order to become an altar for the offering of a sacrifice of pure love and praise and reverence to God must first accomplish these three tasks perfectly. First, they must cast out strange gods, all alien affections and attachments. Second, by denying these appetites and repenting of them—through the dark night of the senses—they must purify themselves of the residue. Third, in order to reach the top of this high mount, their garments must be changed. By means of the first two works, God will substitute new garments for the old. The soul will be clothed in a new understanding of God in God (through removal of the old understanding) and in a new love of God in God, once the will is stripped of all the old cravings and satisfactions. And God will vest the soul with new knowledge when the other old ideas and images are cast aside. He causes all that is of the old self, the abilities of one's natural being, to cease, and he attires all the faculties with new supernatural abilities. As a result, one's activities, once human, now become divine. This is achieved in the state of union when the soul, in which God alone dwells, has no other function than that of an altar on which God is adored in praise and love.

God allows nothing else to dwell together with him. We read, consequently, in 1 Kings that when the Philistines put the ark of the covenant in a temple with their idol, the idol was hurled to the ground at the dawn of each day and broken into pieces. The only appetite God permits and wants in his dwelling place is the desire for the perfect fulfillment of his law and the carrying of the cross of Christ. Scripture teaches that God ordered nothing else to be placed in the ark where the manna was than the Law and the rod of Moses (signifying the cross). Those who have no other goal than the perfect observance of the Lord's law and the carrying of the cross of Christ will be true arks, and they will bear within themselves the real manna, which is God, when they possess perfectly, without anything else, this law and this rod.

CLIMBING THE MOUNTAIN

From The Ascent of Mount Carmel, Book 1,
Chapter 13, Sections 3–13

*Here John spells out what detachment from creatures and
sensory gratification involves. In doing so he quotes some of
the annotations from the sketch "The Mount of Perfection."*

First, have habitual desire to imitate Christ in all your
deeds by bringing your life into conformity with his.
You must then study his life in order to know how to
imitate him and behave in all events as he would.

Second, in order to be successful in this imitation, renounce and remain empty of any sensory satisfaction that is not purely for the honor and glory of
God. Do this out of love for Jesus Christ. In his life
he had no other gratification, nor desired any other,
than the fulfillment of his Father's will, which he
called his meat and food.

For example, if you are offered the satisfaction
of hearing things that have no relation to the service
and glory of God, do not desire this pleasure or the
hearing of these things. When you have an opportunity for the gratification of looking upon objects that
will not help you love God more, do not desire this
gratification of sight. And if in speaking there is a
similar opportunity, act in the same way. And so on
with all the senses insofar as you can duly avoid such

satisfaction. If you cannot except the experience of this satisfaction, it will be sufficient to have no desire for it.

By this method you should endeavor, then, to leave the senses as though in darkness, mortified and empty of that satisfaction. With such vigilance you will gain a great deal in a short time.

Many blessings flow when the four natural passions (joy, hope, fear, and sorrow) are in harmony and at peace. The following maxims contain a complete method for mortifying and pacifying them. If put into practice these maxims will give rise to abundant merit and great virtues.

> Endeavor to be inclined always:
> not to the easiest, but to the most difficult;
> not to the most delightful, but to the most distasteful;
> not to the most gratifying, but to the less pleasant;
> not to what means rest for you, but to hard work;
> not to the consoling, but to the unconsoling;
> not to the most, but to the least;
> not to the highest and most precious, but to the lowest and most despised;
> not to wanting something, but to wanting nothing.

Do not go about looking for the best of temporal things, but for the worst, and, for Christ, desire to enter into complete nakedness, emptiness, and poverty in everything in the world.

You should embrace these practices earnestly and try to overcome the repugnance of your will toward them. If you sincerely put them into practice with order and discretion, you will discover in them great delight and consolation.

These counsels if truly carried out are sufficient for entry into the night of senses. But, to ensure that we give abundant enough counsel, here is another exercise that teaches mortification of concupiscence of the flesh, concupiscence of the eyes, and pride of life, which, as Saint John says, reign in the world and give rise to all the other appetites.

First, try to act with contempt for yourself and desire that all others do likewise.

Second, endeavor to speak in contempt of yourself and desire all others to do so.

Third, try to think lowly and contemptuously of yourself and desire that all others do the same.

As a conclusion to these counsels and rules it would be appropriate to repeat the verses in The Ascent of the Mount, which are instructions for climbing to the summit, the high state of union. Although in the drawing we admittedly refer to the spiritual and interior aspect, we also deal with the spirit of imperfection existent in the sensory and exterior part of the soul, as is evident by the two ways, one on each side of the path that leads to perfection. Consequently these verses will here bear reference to the sensory part. Afterward, in the second division of this night, they may be interpreted in relationship to the spiritual part.

The verses are:

To reach satisfaction in all
desire satisfaction in nothing.
To come to possess all
desire the possession of nothing.
To arrive at being all
desire to be nothing.
To come to the knowledge of all
desire the knowledge of nothing.

To come to enjoy what you have not
you must go by a way in which you enjoy not.
To come to the knowledge you have not
you must go by a way in which you know not.
To come to the possession you have not
you must go by a way in which you possess not.
To come to be what you are not
you must go by a way in which you are not.

When you delay in something
you cease to rush toward the all.
For to go from the all to the all
you must deny yourself of all in all.

And when you come to the possession of the all you must possess it without wanting anything. Because if you desire to have something in all your treasure in God is not purely your all.

In this nakedness the spirit finds its quietude and rest. For in coveting nothing, nothing tires it by pulling it up and nothing oppresses it by pushing it down, because it is in the center of its humility. When it covets something, by this very fact it tires itself.

THE NATURE OF UNION WITH GOD

From *The Ascent of Mount Carmel*, Book 2, Chapter 5,
Sections 3–4, 6–7

In the second book of The Ascent, John moves from dis-
cussing detachment (the first part of the dark night or night
of the senses) to faith (the second part or night of the spirit).
Since the stated purpose of passing through the dark night is
to reach union with God, John pauses to explain what he
means by such union.

To understand the nature of this union, one should
first know that God sustains every soul and dwells in
it substantially, even though it may be that of the
greatest sinner in the world. This union between God
and creatures always exists. By it he conserves their
being so that if the union should end they would
immediately be annihilated and cease to exist. Consequently, in discussing union with God we are not discussing the substantial union that always exists, but
the soul's union with and transformation in God that
does not always exist, except when there is likeness of
love. We will call it the union of likeness; and the former, the essential or substantial union. The union of
likeness is supernatural; the other, natural. The supernatural union exists when God's will and the soul's
are in conformity, so that nothing in the one is repugnant to the other. When the soul rids itself completely

of what is repugnant and unconformed to the divine will, it rests transformed in God through love.

Ridding oneself of what is repugnant to God's will should be understood not only of one's acts but of one's habits as well. Not only must actual voluntary imperfections cease, but habitual imperfections must be annihilated too.

No creature, none of its actions and abilities, can reach or encompass God's nature. Consequently, a soul must strip itself of everything pertaining to creatures and of its actions and abilities (of its understanding, satisfaction, and feeling) so that when everything unlike and unconformed to God is cast out, it may receive the likeness of God. And the soul will receive this likeness because nothing contrary to the will of God will be left in it. Thus it will be transformed in God.

It is true that God is ever present in the soul, as we said, and thereby bestows and preserves its natural being by his sustaining presence. Yet he does not always communicate supernatural being to it. He communicates supernatural being only through love and grace, which not all souls possess. And those who do, do not possess them in the same degree. Some have attained higher degrees of love; others remain in lower degrees. To the soul that is more advanced in love, more conformed to the divine will, God communicates himself more. A person who has reached complete conformity and likeness of will has attained total supernatural union and transformation in God.

Manifestly, then, the more that individuals through attachment and habit are clothed with their own abilities and with creatures, the less disposed they are for this union. For they do not afford God full opportunity to transform their souls into the supernatural. As a result, individuals have nothing more to do than to strip their souls of these natural contraries and dissimilarities so that God, who is naturally communicating himself to them through nature, may do so supernaturally through grace.

Here is an example that will provide a better understanding of this explanation. A ray of sunlight shining on a smudgy window is unable to illumine that window completely and transform it into its own light. It could do this if the window were cleaned and polished. The less the film and stains are wiped away, the less the window will be illumined; and the cleaner the window is, the brighter will be its illumination. The extent of illumination is not dependent on the ray of sunlight but on the window. If the window is totally clean and pure, the sunlight will so transform and illumine it that to all appearances the window will be identical with the ray of sunlight and shine just as the sun's ray. Although obviously the nature of the window is distinct from that of the sun's ray (even if the two seem identical), we can assert that the window is the ray or light of the sun by participation. The soul on which the divine light of God's being is ever shining, or better, in which it is ever dwelling by nature, is like this window, as we have affirmed.

A soul makes room for God by wiping away all the smudges and smears of creatures, by uniting its will perfectly to God's; for to love is to labor to divest and deprive oneself for God of all that is not God. When this is done the soul will be illumined by and transformed in God. And God will so communicate his supernatural being to the soul that it will appear to be God himself and will possess what God himself possesses.

When God grants this supernatural favor to the soul, so great a union is that all the things of both God and the soul become one in participant transformation, and the soul appears to be God more than a soul. Indeed, it is God by participation. Yet truly, its being (even though transformed) is naturally as distinct from God's as it was before, just as the window, although illuminated by the ray, has being distinct from the ray's.

# spiritual
detachment

From *The Ascent of Mount Carmel*, Book 2, Chapter 7,
Sections 4, 5, 8

---

*Our activity during the night of the spirit is to detach our-
selves from our need for spiritual feelings and consolations—
to learn to love God for God alone, not for how God blesses
us or makes us feel.*

Obviously one's journey must not merely exclude the
hindrance of creatures but also embody a dispossession and annihilation in the spiritual part of one's
nature. Our Lord, for our instruction and guidance
along this road, imparted that wonderful teaching—I
think it is possible to affirm that the more necessary
the doctrine the less it is practiced by spiritual persons—that I will quote fully and explain in its genuine and spiritual sense because of its importance and
relevance to our subject. He states in the eighth chapter of Saint Mark: "If any want to become my followers, let them deny themselves and take up their
cross and follow me. For those who want to save their
life will lose it, and those who lose their life for my
sake, and for the sake of the gospel, will save it."

Oh, who can make this counsel of our Savior on
self-denial understandable, and practicable, and
attractive, that spiritual persons might become aware
of the difference between the method many of them
think is good and the one that ought to be used in

traveling this road! They are of the opinion that any kind of withdrawal from the world or reformation of life suffices. Some are content with a certain degree of virtue, perseverance in prayer, and mortification, but never achieve the nakedness, poverty, selflessness, or spiritual purity (which are all the same) about which the Lord counsels us here. For they still feed and clothe their natural selves with spiritual feelings and consolations instead of divesting and denying themselves of these for God's sake. They think denial of self in worldly matters is sufficient without annihilation and purification in the spiritual domain. It happens that, when some of this solid, perfect food (the annihilation of all sweetness in God—the pure spiritual cross and nakedness of Christ's poverty of spirit) is offered them in dryness, distaste, and trial, they run from it as from death and wander about in search only of sweetness and delightful communications from God. Such an attitude is not the hallmark of self-denial and nakedness of spirit but the indication of a spiritual sweet tooth. Through this kind of conduct they become, spiritually speaking, enemies of the cross of Christ.

A genuine spirit seeks rather the distasteful in God than the delectable, leans more toward suffering than toward consolation, more toward dryness and affliction than toward sweet consolation. It knows that this is the significance of following Christ and denying self, that the other method is perhaps a seeking of self in God—something entirely contrary to love. Seeking oneself in God is the same as looking for the caresses and consolations of God. Seeking God in oneself entails not only the desire to do without these consolations for God's sake, but also the inclination to choose for love of Christ all that is most distasteful whether in God or in the world; and this is what loving God means.

I should like to persuade spiritual persons that the road leading to God does not entail a multiplicity of considerations, methods, manners, and experiences—though in their own way these may be a requirement for beginners—but demands only the one thing necessary: true self-denial, exterior and interior, through the surrender of self both to suffering for Christ and to annihilation in all things. In the exercise of this self-denial everything else, and even more, is discovered and accomplished. If one fails in this exercise, the root and sum total of all the virtues, the other methods would amount to no more than going around in circles without getting anywhere, even were one to enjoy considerations and communications as lofty as those of the angels.

A person makes progress only by imitating Christ, who is the Way, the Truth, and the Life. No one goes to the Father but through him, as he states himself in Saint John. Accordingly, I would not consider any spirituality worthwhile that wants to walk in sweetness and ease and run from the imitation of Christ.

OPENNESS TO A NEW KIND OF PRAYER

From *The Ascent of Mount Carmel*, Book 2, Chapter 12, Sections 6–8

One of the turning points in the dark night of the spirit is God's call to move to contemplative prayer, prayer that abides in God's presence without the intellectual activity of meditation on a scriptural passage or event. Here John discusses the need to be open to this call.

Many spiritual persons, after having exercised themselves in approaching God through images, forms, and meditations suitable for beginners, err greatly if they do not determine, dare, or know how to detach themselves from these palpable methods to which they are accustomed. For God then wishes to lead them to more spiritual, interior, and invisible graces by removing the gratification derived from discursive meditation. They still try to hold on to these methods, desiring to travel the road of consideration and meditation, using images as before. They think they must always act in this way. Striving hard to meditate, they draw out little satisfaction or none at all. Rather, aridity, fatigue, and restlessness of soul increase in the measure they strive through meditation for that former sweetness, now unobtainable. They will no longer taste that sensible food, as we said, but rather will enjoy another food, more delicate, interior, and spiritual. Not by working with the imagination will they acquire this spiritual nourishment but by pacifying the soul, by leaving it to its more spiritual quiet and repose.

The more spiritual they are, the more they discontinue trying to make particular acts with their faculties, for they become more engrossed in one general, pure act. Once the faculties reach the end of their journey, they cease to work, just as we cease to walk when we reach the end of our journey. If everything consisted in going, one would never arrive; and if everywhere we found means, when and where could we enjoy the end and goal?

It is sad to see many disturb the soul when it desires to abide in this calm and repose of interior quietude, where it is filled with God's peace and refreshment. Desiring to make it retrace its steps and turn back from the goal in which it now reposes, they draw the soul out to more exterior activity, to considerations, which are the means. They do this with strong repugnance and reluctance in the soul. The soul wants to remain in that peace, which it does not understand, as in its rightful place. People suffer if, after laboring to reach their place of rest, they are forced to return to their labors.

Since these individuals do not understand the mystery of this new experience, they imagine themselves to be idle and doing nothing. Thus in their struggle with considerations and discursive meditations they disturb their quietude. They become filled with aridity and trial because of efforts to get satisfaction by means no longer apt. We can say that the more intense their efforts, the less will be their gain. The more they persist at meditation, the worse their state becomes because they drag the soul farther away from spiritual peace. They resemble one who abandons the greater for the lesser, turns back on a road already covered and wants to redo what is already done.

The proper advice for these individuals is that they must learn to abide in that quietude with a loving attentiveness to God and pay no heed to the imagination and its work. At this stage, as was said, the faculties are at rest and do not work actively but passively, by receiving what God is effecting in them. If at times the soul puts the faculties to work, it should not use excessive efforts or studied reasonings, but it should proceed with gentleness of love, moved more by God than by its own abilities, as we will explain later.

This explanation should be sufficient at present for those who want to make progress. They will understand the appropriateness and necessity of detaching oneself at the required time and season from all these methods, ways, and uses of the imagination.

THE PRAYER OF BEGINNERS

From *The Dark Night of the Soul*, Book 1, Chapter 1

The Ascent ends abruptly in the midst of a discussion of purifying the will during the active night of the spirit. In The Dark Night of the Soul, written in 1584–85, John begins a new discussion of the dark night. He starts by describing those who are just beginning to pray with regular times of meditation.

Souls begin to enter this dark night when God, gradually drawing them out of the state of beginners (those who practice meditation on the spiritual road), begins to place them in the state of proficients (those who are already contemplatives), so that by passing through this state they might reach that of the perfect, which is the divine union of the soul with God. We should first mention here some characteristics of beginners, for the sake of a better explanation and understanding of the nature of this night and of God's motive for placing the soul in it. Although our treatment of these things will be as brief as possible, it will help beginners understand the feebleness of their state and take courage and desire that God place them in this night where the soul is strengthened in virtue and fortified for the inestimable delights of the love of God. And, although we will be delayed for a moment, it will be for no longer than our discussion of this dark night requires.

It should be known, then, that God nurtures and caresses the soul, after it has been resolutely converted to his service, like a loving mother who warms her child with the heat of her bosom, nurses it with good milk and tender food, and carries and caresses it in her arms. But as the child grows older, the mother withholds her caresses and hides her tender love; she rubs bitter aloes on her sweet breast and sets the child down from her arms, letting it walk on its own feet so that it may put aside the habits of childhood and grow accustomed to greater and more important things. The grace of God acts just as a loving mother by re-engendering in the soul new enthusiasm and fervor in the service of God. With no effort on the soul's part, this grace causes it to taste sweet and delectable milk and to experience intense satisfaction in the performance of spiritual exercises, because God is handing the breast of his tender love to the soul, just as if it were a delicate child.

The soul finds its joy, therefore, in spending lengthy periods at prayer, perhaps even entire nights; its penances are pleasures; its fasts, happiness; and the sacraments and spiritual conversations are its consolations. Although spiritual persons do practice these exercises with great profit and persistence, and are very careful about them, spiritually speaking, they conduct themselves in a very weak and imperfect manner. Since their motivation in their spiritual works and exercises is the consolation and satisfaction they experience in them, and since they have not been conditioned by the arduous struggle of practicing virtue, they possess many faults and imperfections in the discharge of their spiritual activities. Assuredly, since everyone's actions are in direct conformity with the habit of perfection that has been acquired, and since these persons have not had time to acquire those firm habits, their work must of necessity be feeble, like that of weak children. For a clearer understanding of this and of how truly imperfect beginners are, insofar as they practice virtue readily because of the satisfaction attached to it, we will describe, using the seven capital vices as our basis, some of the numerous imperfections beginners commit. Thus we will clearly see how very similar their deeds are to those of children. The benefits of the dark night will become evident, since it cleanses and purifies the soul of all these imperfections.

# spiritual pride

From *The Dark Night of the Soul*, Book 1, Chapter 2, Sections 1–7

John explains the traps beginners can fall into as spiritual analogues of the seven deadly sins: pride, avarice, lust, anger, gluttony, envy, and sloth. Here he discusses spiritual pride.

These beginners feel so fervent and diligent in their spiritual exercises and undertakings that a certain kind of secret pride is generated in them that begets a complacency with themselves and their accomplishments, even though holy works do of their very nature cause humility. Then they develop a somewhat vain — at times very vain — desire to speak of spiritual things in others' presence, and sometimes even to instruct rather than be instructed; in their hearts they condemn others who do not seem to have the kind of devotion they would like them to have, and sometimes they give expression to this criticism like the Pharisee who despised the publican while he boasted and praised God for the good deeds he himself accomplished.

The devil, desiring the growth of pride and presumption in these beginners, often increases their fervor and readiness to perform such works, and other ones, too. For he is quite aware that all these works and virtues are not only worthless for them, but even become vices. Some of these persons become so evil-minded that they do not want anyone except themselves to appear holy. By both word and deed they condemn and detract others whenever the occasion arises, seeing the little splinter in their brother's eye and failing to consider the wooden beam in their own eye; they strain at the other's gnat and swallow their own camel.

And when at times their spiritual directors, their confessors, or their superiors disapprove their spirit and method of procedure, they feel that these directors do not understand, or perhaps that this failure to approve derives from a lack of holiness, since they want these directors to regard their conduct with esteem and praise. So they quickly search for some other spiritual advisor more to their liking, someone who will congratulate them and be impressed by their deeds; and they flee, as they would death, those who attempt to place them on the safe road by forbidding these things—and sometimes they even become hostile toward such spiritual directors. Frequently, in their presumption, they make many resolutions but accomplish very little. Sometimes they want others to recognize their spirit and devotion, and as a result occasionally contrive to make some manifestations of it, such as movements, sighs, and other ceremonies; sometimes, with the assistance of the devil, they experience raptures, more often in public than in private, and they are quite pleased, and often eager, for others to take notice of these.

Sometimes they minimize their faults, and at other times they become discouraged by them, since they felt they were already saints, and they become impatient and angry with themselves, which is yet another fault. They are often extremely anxious that God remove their faults and imperfections, but their motive is personal peace rather than God. They fail to realize that were God to remove their faults they might very well become more proud and presumptuous. They dislike praising anyone else, but they love to receive praise, and sometimes they even seek it. In this they resemble the foolish virgins who had to seek oil from others when their own lamps were extinguished.

But souls who are advancing in perfection at this time act in an entirely different manner and with a different quality of spirit. They receive great benefit from their humility, by which they not only place little importance on their deeds, but also take very little self-satisfaction from them. They think everyone else is far better than they are, and usually possess a holy envy of them and would like to emulate their service of God. Since they are truly humble, their growing fervor and the increased number of their good deeds and the gratification they receive from them only cause them to become more aware of their debt to God and the inadequacy of their service to him, and thus the more they do, the less satisfaction they derive from it. Their charity and love make them want to do so much for God that what they actually do accomplish seems as nothing. This loving solicitude goads them, preoccupies them, and absorbs them to such an extent that they never notice what others do or do not accomplish, but if they should, they then think, as I say, that everyone is better than they. They think they themselves are insignificant, and want others to think this also and to belittle and slight their deeds. Moreover, even though others do praise and value their works, these souls are unable to believe them; such praises seem strange to them.

These souls humbly and tranquilly long to be taught by anyone who might be a help to them. This desire is the exact opposite of that other desire we mentioned above, of those who want to be themselves the teachers in everything. When these others notice that someone is trying to give them some instruction, they themselves take the words from their very mouths as though they already know everything. Yet these humble souls, far from desiring to be anyone's teacher, are ready to take a road different from the one they are following, if told to do so. For they do not believe they could ever be right themselves. They rejoice when others receive praise, and their only sorrow is that they do not serve God as these others do. Because they consider their deeds insignificant, they do not want to make them known. They are even ashamed to speak of them to their spiritual directors because they think these deeds are not worth mentioning. They are more eager to speak of their faults and sins, and reveal these to others, than of their virtues. They have an inclination to seek direction from one who will have less esteem for their spirit and deeds. Such is the characteristic of a pure and simple and true spirit, one very pleasing to God. Since the wise Spirit of God dwells within these humble souls, he moves them to keep these treasures hidden, and to manifest only their faults. God gives this grace to the humble, together with the other virtues, just as he denies it to the proud.

SPIRITUAL GLUTTONY

From *The Dark Night of the Soul*, Book 1, Chapter 6, Sections 1, 5–8

Here John discusses spiritual gluttony as seeking sweetness through prayer, worship, and other devotional activities.

A great deal can be said on spiritual gluttony, the fourth vice. There are hardly any persons among these beginners, no matter how excellent their conduct, who do not fall into some of the many imperfections of this vice. These imperfections arise because of the delight beginners find in their spiritual exercises. Many, lured by the delight and satisfaction procured in their religious practices, strive more for spiritual savor than for spiritual purity and discretion; yet it is this purity and discretion that God looks for and finds acceptable throughout a soul's entire spiritual journey. Besides the imperfection of seeking after these delights, the sweetness these persons experience makes them go to extremes and pass beyond the mean in which virtue resides and is acquired. Some, attracted by the delight they feel in their spiritual exercises, kill themselves with penances, and others weaken themselves by fasts and, without the counsel or command of another, overtax their weakness; indeed, they try to hide these penances from the one to whom they owe obedience in such matters. Some even dare perform these penances contrary to obedience.

In receiving Communion they spend all their time trying to get some feeling and satisfaction rather than humbly praising and reverencing God dwelling within them. And they go about this in such a way that, if they do not procure any sensible feeling and satisfaction, they think they have accomplished nothing. As a result they judge very poorly of God and fail to understand that the sensory benefits are the least among those that this most blessed sacrament bestows, for the invisible grace it gives is a greater blessing. God often withdraws sensory delight and pleasure so that souls might set the eyes of faith on this invisible grace. Not only in receiving Communion, but in other spiritual exercises as well, beginners desire to feel God and taste him as if he were comprehensible and accessible. This desire is a serious imperfection and, because it involves impurity of faith, is opposed to God's way.

They have the same defect in their prayer, for they think the whole matter of prayer consists in looking for sensory satisfaction and devotion. They strive to procure this by their own efforts, and tire and weary their heads and their faculties. When they do not get this sensible comfort, they become very disconsolate and think they have done nothing. Because of their aim they lose true devotion and spirit, which lie in distrust of self and in humble and patient perseverance so as to please God. Once they do not find delight in prayer, or in any other spiritual exercise, they feel extreme reluctance and repugnance in returning to it and sometimes even give it up. For after all, as was mentioned, they are like children who are prompted to act not by reason but by pleasure. All their time is spent looking for satisfaction and spiritual consolation; they can never read enough spiritual books, and one minute they are meditating on one subject and the next on another, always hunting for some gratification in the things of God. God very rightly and discreetly and lovingly denies this satisfaction to these beginners. If he did not, they would fall into innumerable evils because of their spiritual gluttony and craving for sweetness. This is why it is important for these beginners to enter the dark night and be purged of this childishness.

Those who are inclined toward these delights have also another serious imperfection, which is that they are weak and remiss in treading the rough way of the cross. A soul given up to pleasure naturally feels aversion toward the bitterness of self-denial.

These people incur many other imperfections because of this spiritual gluttony, of which the Lord in time will cure them through temptations, aridities, and other trials, which are all a part of the dark night. So as not to be too lengthy, I do not want to discuss these imperfections any more, but only point out that spiritual sobriety and temperance beget another very different quality, one of mortification, fear, and sub-missiveness in all things. Individuals thereby become aware that the perfection and value of their works do not depend on quantity or the satisfaction found in them but on knowing how to practice self-denial in them. These beginners ought to do their part in striv-ing after this self-denial until God in fact brings them into the dark night and purifies them. In order to get to our discussion of this dark night, I am passing over these imperfections hurriedly.

SIGNS OF GOD'S CALL TO CONTEMPLATION

From *The Dark Night of the Soul*, Book 1, Chapter 9

Again John discusses the soul's need to move beyond medita-
tion to contemplation. Here he gives some of the signs that
God is calling the soul to make in this transition.

Because these aridities may not proceed from the sensory night and purgation, but from sin and imperfection, or weakness and lukewarmness, or some bad
humor or bodily indisposition, I will give some signs
here for discerning whether the dryness is the result
of this purgation or of one of these other defects. I
find there are three principal signs for knowing this.

The first is that since these souls do not get satisfaction or consolation from the things of God, they do
not get any from creatures either. Since God puts a
soul in this dark night in order to dry up and purge its
sensory appetite, he does not allow it to find sweetness
or delight in anything. Through this sign it can in all
likelihood be inferred that this dryness and distaste is
not the outcome of newly committed sins and imperfections. If this were so, some inclination or propen-
sity to look for satisfaction in something other than
the things of God would be felt in the sensory part,
for when the appetite is allowed indulgence in some
imperfection, the soul immediately feels an inclination
toward it, little or great in proportion to the degree of

its satisfaction and attachment. Yet, because the want of satisfaction in earthly or heavenly things could be the product of some indisposition or melancholic humor, which frequently prevents one from being satisfied with anything, the second sign or condition is necessary.

The second sign for the discernment of this purgation is that the memory ordinarily turns to God solicitously and with painful care, and the soul thinks it is not serving God but turning back, because it is aware of this distaste for the things of God. There is a notable difference between dryness and lukewarmness. The lukewarm are very lax and remiss in their will and spirit, and have no solicitude about serving God. Those suffering from the purgative dryness are ordinarily solicitous, concerned, and pained about not serving God. Even though the dryness may be furthered by melancholia or some other humor — as it often is — it does not thereby fail to produce its purgative effect in the appetite, for the soul will be deprived of every satisfaction and concerned only about God. If this humor is the entire cause, everything ends in displeasure and does harm to one's nature, and there are none of these desires to serve God that accompany the purgative dryness. Even though in this purgative dryness the sensory part of the soul is very cast down, slack, and feeble in its actions because of the little satisfaction it finds, the spirit is ready and strong.

The reason for this dryness is that God transfers his goods and strength from sense to spirit. Since the sensory part of the soul is incapable of the goods of spirit, it remains deprived, dry, and empty. Thus, while the spirit is tasting, the flesh tastes nothing at all and becomes weak in its work. But through this nourishment the spirit grows stronger and more alert, and becomes more solicitous than before about not failing God. If in the beginning the soul does not experience this spiritual savor and delight, but dryness and distaste, the reason is the novelty involved in this exchange. Since its palate is accustomed to these other sensory tastes, the soul still sets its eyes on them. And since, also, its spiritual palate is neither purged nor accommodated for so subtle a taste, it is unable to experience the spiritual savor and good until gradually prepared by means of this dark and obscure night.

Yet, as I say, when these aridities are the outcome of the purgative way of the sensory appetite, the spirit feels the strength and energy to work, which are obtained from the substance of that interior food, even though in the beginning it may not experience the savor, for the reason just mentioned. This food is the beginning of a contemplation that is dark and dry to the senses. Ordinarily this contemplation, which is secret and hidden from the very one who receives it, imparts to the soul, together with the dryness and emptiness it produces in the senses, an inclination to remain alone and in quietude. And the soul will be unable to dwell on any particular thought, nor will it have the desire to do so. If those in whom this occurs know how to remain quiet, without care or solicitude about any interior or exterior work, they will soon in that unconcern and idleness delicately experience the interior nourishment. If the soul desires or tries to experience it, it cannot do so. It is like air that escapes when one tries to grasp it in one's hand.

Now in this state of contemplation, when the soul leaves discursive meditation and enters the state of proficients, it is God who works in it. He therefore binds the interior faculties and leaves no support in the intellect, nor satisfaction in the will, nor remembrance in the memory. At this time a person's own efforts are of no avail, but are an obstacle to the interior peace and work God is producing in the spirit through that dryness of sense. Since this peace is something spiritual and delicate, its fruit is quiet, delicate, solitary, satisfying, and peaceful, and far removed from all the other gratifications of beginners, which are very palpable and sensory.

The third sign follows from this one: the powerlessness, in spite of one's efforts, to meditate and make use of the imagination, the interior sense, as was one's previous custom. At this time God does not communicate through the senses as before, by means of the discursive analysis and synthesis of ideas, but begins to communicate through pure spirit by an act of simple contemplation in which there is no discursive succession of thought. The exterior and interior senses of the lower part of the soul cannot attain to this contemplation. As a result the imaginative power and phantasy can no longer rest in any consideration or find support in it.

From the third sign it can be deduced that this dissatisfaction of the faculties is not the fruit of any bad humor. If it were, people would be able with a little care to return to their former exercises and find support for their faculties when that humor passed away, for it is by its nature changeable. In the purgation of the appetite this return is not possible, because on entering it the powerlessness to meditate always continues. It is true, though, that at times in the beginning the purgation of some souls is not continuous in such a way that they are always deprived of sensory satisfaction and the ability to meditate. Perhaps, because of their weakness, they cannot be weaned all at once. Nevertheless, if they are to advance, they will ever enter farther into the purgation and leave farther behind their work of the senses.

ACCEPTING GOD'S GUIDANCE

From *The Dark Night of the Soul*, Book 1, Chapter 10

Here John emphasizes that spiritual progress is at God's direction, not our own, and in God's own time. We need to understand how God leads the soul to avoid becoming impatient or turning back from God's call.

At the time of the aridities of this sensory night, God makes the exchange we mentioned by withdrawing the soul from the life of the senses and placing it in that of spirit—that is, he brings it from meditation to contemplation—where the soul no longer has the power to work or meditate with its faculties on the things of God. Spiritual persons suffer considerable affliction in this night, owing not so much to the aridities they undergo as to their fear of having gone astray. Since they do not find any support or satisfaction in good things, they believe there will be no more spiritual blessings for them and that God has abandoned them. They then grow weary and strive, as was their custom, to concentrate their faculties with some satisfaction on a subject of meditation, and they think that if they do not do this and do not feel that they are at work, they are doing nothing. This effort of theirs is accompanied by an interior reluctance and repugnance on the part of the soul, for it would be pleased to dwell in that quietude and idleness without working with the faculties. They consequently impair God's work and do not profit by their own. In searching for spirit, they lose the spirit that was the source of their tranquillity and peace. They are like someone who turns from what has already been done in order to do it again, or like one who leaves a city only to re-enter it, or they are like a hunter who abandons the prey in order to go hunting again. It is useless, then, for the soul to try to meditate because it will no longer profit by this exercise.

If there is no one to understand these persons, they either turn back and abandon the road or lose courage, or at least they hinder their own progress because of their excessive diligence in treading the path of discursive meditation. They fatigue and overwork themselves, thinking that they are failing because of their negligence or sins. Meditation is now useless for them because God is conducting them along another road, which is contemplation and is very different from the first, for the one road belongs to discursive meditation and the other is beyond the range of the imagination and discursive reflection.

Those who are in this situation should feel comforted; they ought to persevere patiently and not be afflicted. Let them trust in God who does not fail those who seek him with a simple and righteous heart; nor will he fail to impart what is needful for the way until getting them to the clear and pure light of love. God will give them this light by means of that other night, the night of spirit, if they merit that he place them in it. The attitude necessary in the night of sense is to pay no attention to discursive meditation since this is not the time for it. They should allow the soul to remain in rest and quietude even though it may seem obvious to them that they are doing nothing and wasting time, and even though they think this disinclination to think about anything is due to their laxity. Through patience and perseverance in prayer, they will be doing a great deal without activity on their part. All that is required of them here is freedom of soul, that they liberate themselves from the impediment and fatigue of ideas and thoughts, and care not about thinking and meditating. They must be content simply with a loving and peaceful attentiveness to God, and live without the concern, without the effort, and without the desire to taste or feel him. All these desires disquiet the soul and distract it from the peaceful, quiet, and sweet idleness of the contemplation that is being communicated to it.

And even though more scruples come to the fore concerning the loss of time and the advantages of doing something else, since it cannot do anything or think of anything in prayer, the soul should endure them peacefully, as though going to prayer means remaining in ease and freedom of spirit. If individuals were to desire to do something themselves with their interior faculties, they would hinder and lose the goods that God engraves on their souls through that peace and idleness. If a model for the painting or retouching of a portrait should move because of a desire to do something, the artist would be unable to finish and the work would be spoiled. Similarly, any operation, affection, or thought a soul might cling to when it wants to abide in interior peace and idleness would cause distraction and disquietude, and make it feel sensory dryness and emptiness. The more a person seeks some support in knowledge and affection the more the soul will feel the lack of these, for this support cannot be supplied through these sensory means.

Accordingly, such persons should not mind if the operations of their faculties are being lost to them; they should desire rather that this be done quickly so they may be no obstacle to the operation of the infused contemplation God is bestowing, so they may receive it with more peaceful plenitude and make room in the spirit for the enkindling and burning of the love that this dark and secret contemplation bears and communicates to the soul. For contemplation is nothing else than a secret and peaceful and loving inflow of God, which, if not hampered, fires the soul in the spirit of love.

PRAYER OF PROFICIENTS

From *The Dark Night of the Soul*, Book 2, Chapters 3–4

At last John is ready to describe the passive night of the spirit. He begins with a description of prayer as experienced by proficients: those who have moved from meditation to contemplation, but are still far from perfection. As part of this, he offers this third explanation of the first stanza of the poem.

These souls, then, are now proficients. Their senses have been fed with sweet communications so that, allured by the gratification flowing from the spirit, they could be accommodated and united to the spirit. These two parts thus united and conformed are jointly prepared to suffer the rough and arduous purgation of the spirit that awaits them. In this purgation, these two portions of the soul will undergo complete purification, for one part is never adequately purged without the other. The real purgation of the senses begins with the spirit. Hence the night of the senses we explained should be called a certain reformation and bridling of the appetite rather than a purgation. The reason is that all the imperfections and disorders of the sensory part are rooted in the spirit and from it receive their strength. All good and evil habits reside in the spirit and until these habits are purged, the senses cannot be completely purified of their rebellions and vices.

In this night that follows both parts are jointly purified. This was the purpose of the reformation of the first night and the calm that resulted from it: that the sensory part, united in a certain way with the spirit, might undergo purgation and suffering with greater fortitude. Such is the fortitude necessary for so strong and arduous a purgation that if the lower part in its weakness is not reformed first, and afterward strengthened in God through the experience of sweet and delightful communion with him, it has neither the fortitude nor the preparedness to endure it.

These proficients are still very lowly and natural in their communion with God and in their activity directed toward him because the gold of the spirit is not purified and illumined. They still think of God and speak of him as little children, and their knowledge and experience of him are like those of little children, as Saint Paul asserts. The reason is that they have not reached perfection, which is union of the soul with God. Through this union, as fully grown, they do mighty works in the spirit since their faculties and works are more divine than human, as we will point out. Wishing to strip them in fact of this old self and clothe them with the new, which is created according to God in the newness of sense, as the Apostle says, God divests the faculties, affections, and senses, both spiritual and sensory, interior and exterior. He leaves the intellect in darkness, the will in aridity, the memory in emptiness, and the affections in supreme affliction, bitterness, and anguish by depriving the soul of the feeling and satisfaction it previously obtained from spiritual blessings. For this privation is one of the conditions required that the spiritual form, which is the union of love, may be introduced into the spirit and united with it. The Lord works all of this in the soul by means of a pure and dark contemplation, as is indicated in the first stanza. Although we explained this stanza in reference to the first night of the senses, the soul understands it mainly in relation to this second night of the spirit, since this night is the principal purification of the soul. With this in mind, we will quote it and explain it again.

> One dark night,
> fired with love's urgent longings
> —ah, the sheer grace!—
> I went out unseen,
> my house being now all stilled.

Understanding this stanza now to refer to contemplative purgation or nakedness and poverty of spirit (which are all about the same), we can thus explain it, as though the soul says: Poor, abandoned, and unsupported by any of the apprehensions of my soul (in the darkness of my intellect, the distress of my will, and the affliction and anguish of my memory), left to darkness in pure faith, which is a dark night for these natural faculties, and with my will touched only by sorrows, afflictions, and longings of love of God, I went out from myself. That is, I departed from my low manner of understanding, and my feeble way of loving, and my poor and limited method of finding satisfaction in God. I did this unhindered by either the flesh or the devil.

This was great happiness and a sheer grace for me, because through the annihilation and calming of my faculties, passions, appetites, and affections, by which my experience and satisfaction in God were base, I went out from my human operation and way of acting to God's operation and way of acting. That is: My intellect departed from itself, changing from human and natural to divine. For united with God through this purgation, it no longer understands by means of its natural vigor and light, but by means of the divine wisdom to which it was united. And my will departed from itself and became divine. United with the divine love, it no longer loves in a lowly manner, with its natural strength, but with the strength and purity of the Holy Spirit; and thus the will does not operate humanly in relation to God. The memory, too, was changed into presentiments of eternal glory. And finally, all the strength and affections of the soul, by means of this night and purgation of the old self, are renewed with divine qualities and delights.

LIGHT IN
THE NIGHT

From *The Dark Night of the Soul*, Book 2, Chapter 9,
Sections 1–4

*In this stage of the dark night, the soul can begin to hope for
dawn and to experience the light of union with God.*

It remains to be said, then, that even though this
happy night darkens the spirit, it does so only to
impart light concerning all things; and even though it
humbles individuals and reveals their miseries, it does
so only to exalt them; and even though it impoverishes
and empties them of all possessions and natural affection, it does so only that they may reach out divinely
to the enjoyment of all earthly and heavenly things,
with a general freedom of spirit in them all. That ele-
ments be commingled with all natural compounds,
they must be unaffected by any particular color, odor,
or taste, and thus they can concur with all colors,
odors, and tastes. Similarly, the spirit must be simple,
pure, and naked as to all natural affections, actual and
habitual, in order to be able to communicate freely in
fullness of spirit with the divine wisdom in which, on
account of the soul's purity, the delights of all things
are tasted to a certain eminent degree. Without this
purgation the soul would be wholly unable to experience the satisfaction of all this abundance of spiritual

delight. Only one attachment or one particular object to which the spirit is actually or habitually bound is enough to hinder the experience or reception of the delicate and intimate delight of the spirit of love that contains eminently in itself all delights.

Because of their one attachment to the food and fleshmeat they had tasted in Egypt, the children of Israel were unable to get any taste from the delicate bread of angels—the manna of the desert, which, as Scripture says, contained all savors and was changed to the taste each one desired. Similarly the spirit, still affected by some actual or habitual attachment or some particular knowledge or any other apprehension, is unable to taste the delights of the spirit of freedom. The reason is that the affections, feelings, and apprehensions of the perfect spirit, because they are divine, are of another sort and are so eminent and so different from the natural that their actual and habitual possession demands the annihilation and expulsion of the natural affections and apprehensions; for two contraries cannot coexist in one subject. Hence, so the soul may pass on to these grandeurs, this dark night of contemplation must necessarily annihilate it first and undo it in its lowly ways by putting it into darkness, dryness, conflict, and emptiness. For the light imparted to the soul is a most lofty divine light that transcends all natural light and does not belong naturally to the intellect.

That the intellect reach union with the divine light and become divine in the state of perfection, this dark contemplation must first purge and annihilate it of its natural light and bring it actually into obscurity. It is fitting that this darkness last as long as is necessary for the expulsion and annihilation of the intellect's habitual way of understanding, which was a long time in use, and that divine light and illumination take its place. Since that strength of understanding was natural to the intellect, the darkness it here suffers is profound, frightful, and extremely painful. This darkness seems to be substantial darkness, since it is felt in the deep substance of the spirit. The affection of love that is bestowed in the divine union of love is also divine, and consequently very spiritual, subtle, delicate, and interior, exceeding every affection and feeling of the will and every appetite. The will, as a result, must first be purged and annihilated of all its affections and feelings in order to experience and taste, through union of love, this divine affection and delight, which is so sublime and does not naturally belong to the will. The soul is left in a dryness and distress proportional to its habitual natural affections (whether for divine or human things), so that every kind of demon may be debilitated, dried up, and tried in the fire of this divine contemplation, as when Tobias placed the fish heart in the fire, and the soul may become pure and simple, with a palate purged and healthy and ready to experience the sublime and marvelous touches of divine love. After the expulsion of all actual and habitual obstacles, it will behold itself transformed in these divine touches.

Furthermore, in this union for which the dark night is a preparation, the soul in its communion with God must be endowed and filled with a certain glorious splendor embodying innumerable delights. These delights surpass all the abundance the soul can possess naturally, for nature, so weak and impure, cannot receive these delights. As a result the soul must first be set in emptiness and poverty of spirit and purged of every natural support, consolation, and apprehension, earthly and heavenly. Thus empty, it is truly poor in spirit and stripped of the old self, and thereby able to live that new and blessed life which is the state of union with God, attained by means of this night.

The Ladder of Love

From *The Dark Night of the Soul*, Book 2,
Chapters 19–20

Near the end of The Dark Night, *John offers another
metaphor of the spiritual journey: a ladder of love reaching
from beginning to union. It is based on a work attributed—
incorrectly—to Bernard of Clairvaux. This selection is
severely abridged in order to show the basic progression of all
ten steps.*

We mentioned that there are ten successive steps on
this ladder of love by which the soul ascends to God.
The first step of love makes the soul sick in an advan-
tageous way. The bride speaks of this step of love
when she says: "I adjure you, O daughters of Jeru-
salem, if you find my beloved, tell him this: I am faint
with love." Yet this sickness is not unto death but for
the glory of God, because in this sickness the soul's
languor pertains to sin and to all the things that are
not God. As a sick person changes color and loses
appetite for all foods, so on this step of love the soul
changes the color of its past life and loses its appetite
for all things. It becomes unable then to find satisfaction, support, consolation, or a resting place in anything. The soul therefore begins immediately to
ascend from this step to the next.

The second step causes a person to search for God unceasingly. When the bride was languishing, she added: "I will rise now and . . . seek him whom my soul loves." Searching for him in all things, it pays heed to nothing until it finds him. Since the soul is here convalescing and gaining strength in the love found in this second step, it immediately begins to ascend to the third through a certain degree of new purgation in the night.

The third step of this loving ladder prompts the soul to the performance of works and gives it fervor that it might not fail. The royal prophet exclaims: "Happy are those who fear the LORD, who greatly delight in his commandments." If fear, a child of love, produces this eagerness in the soul, what will love itself do? On this step the soul thinks the great works it does for the Beloved are small; its many works, few; the long time spent in his service, short. It believes all of this because of the fire of love in which it is now burning. One reason for this effect is that love is teaching them what God deserves; another is that because the works they perform for God are many and they know them to be wanting and imperfect, they are confused and pained by them all. On this third step the soul is far removed from vainglory, presumption, and the practice of condemning others. And thus one acquires the courage and strength to ascend to the fourth step.

On the fourth step of this ladder of love a habitual yet unwearisome suffering is engendered on account of the Beloved. As Saint Augustine says: "Love makes all burdensome and heavy things nearly nothing." The spirit possesses so much energy on this step that it brings the flesh under control and takes as little account of it as would a tree of one of its leaves. The soul in no way seeks consolation or satisfaction either in God or in anything else; neither does it desire or ask favors of God, for it is clearly aware that it has already received many from him. All its care is directed toward how it might give some pleasure to God and render him some service because of what he deserves and the favors he has bestowed, even though the cost might be high.

On the fifth step the desire of the lover to apprehend and be united with the Beloved is so ardent that any delay, no matter how slight, is long, annoying, and tiresome. The soul is ever believing that it is finding its Beloved; and when it sees its desire frustrated, which is at almost every step, it faints in its longing, as the psalmist declares: "My soul longs, indeed it faints for the courts of the LORD." On this step the lover must either see its love or die.

The sixth step makes the soul run swiftly toward God and experience many touches in him. It runs without fainting by reason of its hope. The love that has invigorated it makes it fly swiftly. The prophet Isaiah also speaks of this step: "Those who wait for the LORD shall renew their strength, they shall mount up with wings like eagles, . . . they shall walk and not faint."

The seventh step of the ladder gives the soul an ardent boldness. At this stage love neither profits by the judgment to wait nor makes use of the counsel to retreat, neither can it be curbed through shame. For the favor God now gives it imparts an ardent daring. Hence the Apostle says: "[Love] believes all things, hopes all things, endures all things."

The eighth step of love impels the soul to lay hold of the Beloved without letting go, as the bride proclaims: "I found him whom my soul loves. I held him and would not let him go." Although the soul satisfies its desire on this step of union, it does not do so continually. Some manage to get to it, but soon turn back and leave it. If one were to remain on this step, a certain glory would be possessed in this life, and so the soul rests on it for only short periods of time. After this step comes the ninth, which is that of the perfect.

The ninth step of love causes the soul to burn gently. The Holy Spirit produces this gentle and delightful ardor by reason of the perfect soul's union with God. We cannot speak of the goods and riches of God a person enjoys on this step because even were we to write many books about them the greater part would remain unsaid.

The tenth and last step of this secret ladder of love assimilates the soul to God completely because of the clear vision of God that a person possesses at once on reaching it. After arriving at the ninth step in this life, the soul departs from the body. Saint Matthew says: "Blessed are the pure in heart, for they will see God." As we mentioned, this vision is the cause of the soul's complete likeness to God. Saint John says: "We will be like him," not because the soul will have as much capacity as God — this is impossible — but because all it is will become like God. Thus it will be called, and shall be, God through participation.

Thus, by means of this mystical theology and secret love, the soul departs from itself and all things and ascends to God. For love is like a fire that always rises upward as though longing to be engulfed in its center.

appendix

Reading Spiritual Classics for Personal and Group Formation

Many Christians today are searching for more spiritual depth, for something more than simply being good church members. That quest may send them to the spiritual practices of New Age movements or of Eastern religions such as Zen Buddhism. Christians, though, have their own long spiritual tradition, a tradition rich with wisdom, variety, and depth.

The great spiritual classics testify to that depth. They do not concern themselves with mystical flights for a spiritual elite. Rather, they contain very practical advice and insights that can support and shape the spiritual growth of any Christian. We can all benefit by sitting at the feet of the masters (both male and female) of Christian spirituality.

Reading spiritual classics is different from most of the reading we do. We have learned to read to master a text and extract information from it. We tend to read quickly, to get through a text. And we summarize as we read, seeking the main point. In reading spiritual classics, though, we allow the text to master and form us. Such formative reading goes more slowly, more reflectively, allowing time for God to speak to us through the text. God's word for us may come as easily from a minor point or even an aside as from the major point.

Formative reading requires that you approach the text in humility. Read as a seeker, not an expert. Don't demand that the text meet your expectations for what an "enlightened" author should write. Humility means accepting the author as another imperfect human, a product of his or her own time and situation. Learn to celebrate what is foundational in an author's writing without being overly disturbed by what is peculiar to the author's life and times. Trust the text as a gift from both God and the author, offered to you for your benefit — to help you grow in Christ.

To read formatively, you must also slow down. Feel free to reread a passage that seems to speak specially to you. Stop from time to time to reflect on what you have been reading. Keep a journal for these reflections. Often the act of writing can itself prompt further, deeper reflection. Keep your notebook open and your pencil in hand as you read. You might not get back to that wonderful insight later. Don't worry that you are not getting through an entire passage — or even the first paragraph! Formative reading is about depth rather than breadth, quality rather than quantity. As you read, seek God's direction for your own life. Timeless truths have their place but may not be what is most important for your own formation here and now.

As you read the passage, you might keep some of these questions running through your mind:

- How is what I'm reading true of my own life? Where does it reflect my own *experience*?

- How does this text challenge me? What new *direction* does it offer me?
- What must I change to put what I am reading into practice? How can I *incarnate* it, let this word become flesh in my life?

You might also devote special attention to sections that upset you. What is the source of the disturbance? Do you want to argue theology? Are you turned off by cultural differences? Or have you been skewered by an insight that would turn your life upside down if you took it seriously? Let your journal be a dialogue with the text.

If you find yourself moving from reading the text to chewing over its implications to praying, that's great! Spiritual reading is really the first step in an ancient way of prayer called *lectio divina* or "divine reading." Reading leads naturally into reflection on what you have read (meditation). As you reflect on what the text might mean for your life, you may well want to ask for God's help in living out any new insights or direction you have perceived (prayer). Sometimes such prayer may lead you further into silently abiding in God's presence (contemplation). And, of course, the process is only really completed when it begins to make a difference in the way we live (incarnation).

As good as it is to read spiritual classics in solitude, it is even better to join with others in a small group for mutual formation or "spiritual direction in common." This is *not* the same as a study group that talks about spiritual classics. A group for mutual formation would have similar goals as for an individual's reading: to allow the text to shine its light on the *experiences* of the group members, to suggest new *directions* for their lives and practical ways of *incarnating* these directions. Such a group might agree to focus on one short passage from a classic at each meeting (even if members have read more). Discussion usually goes much deeper if all the members have already read and reflected on the passage before the meeting and bring their journals.

Such groups need to watch for several potential problems. It is easy to go off on a tangent (especially if it takes the focus off the members' own experience and onto generalities). At such times a group leader might bring the group's attention back to the text: "What does our author say about that?" Or, "How do we experience that in our own lives?" When a group member shares a problem, others may be tempted to try to "fix" it. This is much less helpful than sharing similar experiences and how they were handled (for good or ill). "Sharing" someone else's problems (whether that person is in or out of the group) should be strongly discouraged.

One person could be designated as leader, to be responsible for opening and closing prayers; to be the first to share or respond to the text; and to keep notes during the discussion to highlight recurring themes, challenges, directives, or practical steps. These responsibilities could also be shared among several members of the group or rotated.

For further information about formative reading of spiritual classics, try *A Practical Guide to Spiritual Reading* by Susan Annette Muto. *Shaped by the Word* by Robert Mulholland (Upper Room Books®) covers formative reading of the Bible. *Good Things Happen: Experiencing Community in Small Groups* by Dick Westley is an excellent resource on forming small groups of all kinds.